SPIDERS

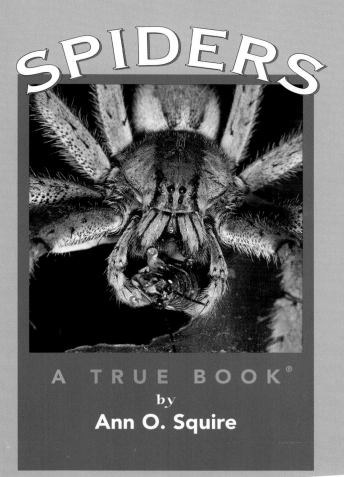

A TRUE BOOK®

by
Ann O. Squire

Children's Press®
A Division of Scholastic Inc.

New York Toronto London Auckland Sydney
Mexico City New Delhi Hong Kong
Danbury, Connecticut

A jumping spider
eating a deer fly

Reading Consultant
Nanci R. Vargus, Ed.D.
*Assistant Professor
Literacy Education
University of Indianapolis
Indianapolis, IN*

Content Consultant
Alan C. York
*Department of Entomology
Purdue University
West Lafayette, IN*

Dedication:
For Emma

*The photo on the cover shows
a crab spider. The photo on
the title page shows a female
wandering spider eating
a cricket.*

Library of Congress Cataloging-in-Publication Data

Squire, Ann.
  Spiders / by Ann O. Squire.
     p. cm. — (A True book)
  Summary: Reveals the physical characteristics and behavior of spiders,
  and describes two spiders commonly found in North America.
  Includes bibliographical references (p.   ).
   ISBN 0-516-22661-4 (lib. bdg.)   0-516-29361-3 (pbk.)
   1. Spiders—Juvenile literature. [1. Spiders.] I. Title. II. Series.
  QL458.4.S678 2003
  595.4'4—dc21

                                        2003008479

© 2003 by Scholastic Inc.
All rights reserved. Published simultaneously in Canada.
Printed in the United States of America.

CHILDREN'S PRESS, and A TRUE BOOK®, and associated logos are
trademarks and or registered trademarks of Scholastic Library Publishing.
SCHOLASTIC and associated logos are trademarks and or registered
trademarks of Scholastic Inc.

1 2 3 4 5 6 7 8 9 10 R 12 11 10 09 08 07 06 05 04 03

Contents

This spider has caught some beetles in its web.

The Spider and the Fly

Have you ever seen a fly trapped in a spider's web? If so, you probably knew what was going to happen to that fly: It would soon become the spider's dinner. Besides the fact that the spider is the hunter and the fly is the victim, you might not think there is much difference between the two. In fact, spiders and other **arachnids** are different in almost every way from flies and other insects.

The easiest difference to spot is the number of legs. All insects have six legs, but spiders have eight. The bodies of insects are divided into three parts (head, thorax, and abdomen), but a spider's body is divided into two parts (cephalothorax and abdomen). Because a spider's head and

All spiders have eight legs (above). A spider's body is divided into the cephalothorax and the abdomen (right).

thorax are joined together, it cannot turn its head from side to side.

A wolf spider has two large eyes and four smaller ones below.

Like insects, spiders have eyes and can see the world. But while insects have two eyes, most spiders have six or eight. Usually their eyes are lined up in several rows on their heads.

Some spiders that actively hunt for food have their eyes arranged so that they can see in nearly every direction at once! Instead of using antennae, a spider feels and tastes things with its **pedipalps**, which are

A spider uses its front legs to hold food.

located in front of its first pair of legs. The pedipalps are sometimes used to help hold and crush food. Once the spider has captured its prey, it uses its sharp, powerful jaws, called **chelicerae**, to bite its victim and inject poisonous venom.

Finally, all spiders have little nozzles, called **spinnerets**, located at the ends of their bodies. Using its spinnerets, a spider can spin a thin, strong thread of silk to create its web. Besides weaving webs, spiders

A spider uses its spinnerets to produce silk.

use silk to line their burrows, make containers for their eggs, and wrap their prey. Some spiders even use their silk like sails to help them move from place to place.

Finding Food: To Web or Not to Web

All spiders are **carnivores** (meat eaters), but different species have very different ways of capturing their prey. Most people are familiar with the large round webs, called orb webs, that garden spiders

Some spiders build orb webs between two sturdy objects.

use to trap their victims. Suspended between two branches or tucked into the corner of a garage or shed, these sticky webs make very good traps for catching flying insects. However, orb webs are easily damaged by bad weather and struggling prey. So, the spider is forced to repair its web or weave a new one nearly every day.

Other spider species capture prey without doing all the work to construct a web. Like a real wolf, the wolf spider is a fast runner with good eyesight. After spotting its victim, the wolf spider creeps toward it

A wolf spider will sneak up on prey and attack it.

slowly and silently. When it is finally close enough, the spider darts forward and grabs the prey in its powerful jaws.

A spitting spider wraps its prey up with its silk.

Spitting spiders also rely on eyesight to help them locate prey. They also use a very unusual weapon. When a spitting spider spots its victim, it takes aim and shoots two streams of sticky liquid through its jaws. At the same time, the spider quickly waggles back and forth, so that the insect is pinned to the ground under a gooey, zigzag net.

When it comes to catching prey, there is no spider quite as strange as the bolas spider. Starting in the early evening, this spider hangs

A bolas spider
hunts by swinging
a sticky ball at the
end of a thread.

from a twig and releases a silk
thread about 2 inches (5 cen-
timeters) long. To the end of
the thread it attaches a sticky

ball, which it dangles in the air. This sticky ball smells like a female moth. As night falls, male moths fly about looking for females. When a male moth comes within range because of the attractive smell, the bolas spider swings its silk ball. If it is lucky, the ball hits its target, and the moth is trapped like a fly on flypaper. Then the bolas spider reels in its catch and kills it with a deadly bite.

Anatomy of a Web

You have probably seen a fat spider sitting at the center of its spiral web. Did you ever wonder how the spider managed to weave such a complicated net? The first step the spider takes to build a web is stringing a thread of silk between two objects. After that, the spider

Spiders begin
their webs by
connecting two
objects with a
strand of silk.

spins the outer circle and the
strong threads that run out-
ward from the center, like the

A spider will wait
for prey in the
center of a web.

spokes of a bicycle wheel. Then, starting at the center, it works its way around and around the web, while releasing a spiral of sticky silk. When the web is complete, the spider rests at the center or off to one side, waiting for vibrations that will tell it an insect has stumbled into its trap and is struggling to free itself.

The orb web may be the most complicated, but it is certainly not the only kind of

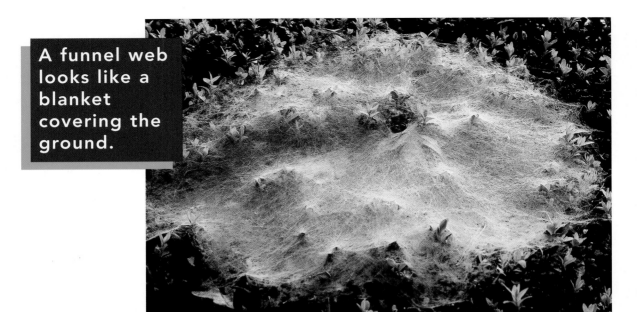

A funnel web looks like a blanket covering the ground.

web that spiders build. The funnel web spider makes a web that looks like a funnel or a saggy sheet. Sometimes the spider adds a tangle of threads just above the sheet. At the edge of the web is a silken tube in which the spider waits for its prey. Soon, an insect flies into the threads, loses its balance, and drops onto the sheet below. When it feels the insect's struggle for freedom, the spider rushes out and grabs the victim.

The spider will hide in the funnel part of the web until prey arrives.

A water spider catches its meals underwater.

Like people, spiders need air to stay alive. The water spider, which lives in ponds and lakes, has an odd problem: How can it breathe air while living underwater? To solve this problem, the water spider spins a web that acts like a miniature diving bell. Then it attaches the bell-shaped web to a weed or plant. The spider swims to the surface, grasps an air bubble with its hind legs, and carries it down to its web. The spider does this over and over until there is a good supply of air under the bell. Then it crawls inside its home and waits.

By trapping air bubbles in its legs and abdomen, the spider is able to fill its underwater web with air.

When an insect or small fish passes by, the water spider darts out, grabs its prey, and drags it inside the bell.

A Sticky Situation

Do you know why spiders never get stuck in their own webs? Only the strands circling the web are sticky, while the spokes that fan out from the center are dry. When moving around the web, the spider is careful to walk only on the spokes.

A spider knows which spokes of the web are safe to walk on.

Having Babies

Mating season can be a dangerous time for male spiders. For one thing, most male spiders are smaller than the females. If the male isn't careful, there is a good chance the female will see him as dinner rather than as a mate. When a male garden

Female spiders are usually much larger than male spiders (above). A male spider will signal a female by tapping on her web (right).

spider visits a female in her web, he needs some kind of signal to let her know that he is not a fly or other prey insect. He sends this message by tapping on the web in a special way that is very different from the vibrations made by a struggling insect. If he is lucky, the female will accept him and the two will mate.

Wait! The male isn't out of danger yet. Even when mating is successful, many female spiders kill and eat their mates. In fact, this is how the black widow spider got its name.

Male black widow spiders might be eaten by female black widows after mating.

In spite of this, spiders are very good mothers. The female surrounds her eggs with a tough, silken egg case, which protects the eggs from enemies. Many spider mothers guard their egg cases until they hatch. Wolf spiders and some other species attach the egg cases to their bodies and carry them around.

When the eggs are ready to hatch, the wolf spider mother bites open the egg case. The baby spiders emerge and climb up their mother's legs onto her back. For the next few days, she will give her babies a free

Mother spiders surround their eggs with a protective silk casing (below). These wolf spiders (right) are catching a ride on their mother's back.

ride until they are old enough to live on their own.

When it is time to leave home, some baby spiders just crawl away. Others climb to the

After they hatch, some baby spiders will release silk and get carried away by the wind.

top of a plant, stand with their abdomens pointing up, and release threads of silk from their spinnerets. Sooner or later, a gust of wind catches the silk and lifts the baby spiders off the ground, carrying them to new homes far away.

Arachnophobia!

Are you afraid of spiders? For most people, furry tarantulas and poisonous black widows are enough to bring on night-mares. For some people, though, this dislike of spiders turns into an abnormal fear called **arachnophobia**. You don't have to worry too much

Some people are afraid to go near spiders.

about being harmed by a spider. The chances of meeting a deadly spider are actually very small. Of the 35,000 species of spiders in the world, only about twelve species are highly poisonous.

Although they are large and hairy, tarantulas are actually shy spiders that are not nearly as poisonous as people think. When defending themselves against enemies, some tarantula species use their hind legs to

This large tarantula may look scary, but it is really not that dangerous.

rub off some of the sharp, barbed hairs that cover their abdomens. If an attacker inhales these hairs or gets them in its eyes, the result can be far more painful than the tarantula's bite.

A tarantula may use the barbed hairs that cover its body as a weapon against attackers.

You can identify a black widow by the red hourglass on its abdomen.

The most poisonous spider in North America is the black widow, which can be recognized by the red hourglass shape on its abdomen.

Although the black widow's venom is fifteen to fifty times more toxic than the venom of a rattlesnake, this spider's bite is rarely fatal. Only a very small amount of venom is injected with each bite.

Black widow spiders spin their tangled webs near the ground. They are most often found in dark crevices or places where objects have been stacked together, such as cluttered garages or wood-piles. Black widows are shy

A black widow will build a web in a quiet place away from people.

and will not bite unless they are disturbed. If you use common sense, and avoid areas where they may be hiding, you'll probably never see a black widow other than in the pages of a book.

To Find Out More

Here are some additional resources to help you learn more about spiders:

 **Books**

Clarke, Penny. **Spiders, Insects, and Minibeasts.** Danbury, CT: Franklin Watts, 2002.

Berger, Melvin. **Do All Spiders Spin Webs?: Questions and Answers About Spiders.** New York: Scholastic Reference, 2000.

Squire, Ann O. **Spiders of North America.** Danbury, CT: Franklin Watts, 2000.

Organizations and Online Sites

http://www.amonline.net. au/spiders/

The website of the Australian museum provides good general information on spiders, and explores the role of spiders in art, history, and culture.

http://members.aol.com/ YESedu/welcome.html/

The website of the Young Entomologists' Society has articles, games, photos, and lots of information on spiders and other insects.

http://www.slsc.org/docs/ online/spiders/index.shtml

This website, from Smithsonian Institution Traveling Exhibition Service, includes craft projects, games, and a reading list on spiders.

Important Words

arachnid any member of the class Arachnida, which includes spiders, scorpions, mites, and ticks

arachnophobia an abnormal fear of arachnids, especially spiders

carnivore an animal that eats other animals

chelicerae the fanglike jaws near a spider's mouth. Chelicerae are often modified for grasping and piercing.

pedipalps the second pair of appendages near the mouth of a spider (behind the chelicerae and in front of the first pair of legs). Pedipalps help the spider to sense the world and grasp food, and are also used in mating.

spinnerets nozzle-like structures at the end of the spider's abdomen that produce silk.

Index

Meet the Author

Ann O. Squire has a Ph.D. in animal behavior. Before becoming a writer, she spent several years studying African electric fish and the special signals they use to communicate with each other. Dr. Squire is the author of many books on animals and natural science topics, including *Ants, Beetles, Crickets and Grasshoppers,* and *Spiders of North America.* She lives with her children, Emma and Evan, in Katonah, New York.

Photographs © 2003: Animals Animals: 16 (C.C. Lockwood), 18 (Bertram G. Murray); Dwight R. Kuhn Photography: cover, 2, 7 bottom, 9, 36, 38; Minden Pictures: 39, 40 (Mark Moffett), 29 (Konrad Wothe); Peter Arnold Inc./Hans Pfletschinger: 31 bottom; Photo Researchers, NY: 22 (Kenneth M. Highfill), 13 (David Hosking), 8 (Tom McHugh), 7 top, 31 top (John Mitchell), 21 (Robert Noonan), 11, 28 (Perennou Nuridsany), 25 (Stephen P. Parker), 15 (Rod Planck), 1, 35 left (David T. Roberts/Nature's Images, Inc.), 33 (James H. Robinson), 43 (Dan Suzio); Visuals Unlimited: 4 (Bill Beatty), 24 (Gary W. Carter), 35 right (Gary Meszaros), 26 (Kjell B. Sandved), 41 (Rob & Ann Simpson)